DEVELOPING YOUR

FIVE

SPIRITUAL

SENSES

DEVELOPING YOUR

FIVE

SPIRITUAL

SENSES

HEAR, SEE, TASTE, SMELL AND TOUCH
the invisible world around you

PATRICIA KING

Developing Your Five Spiritual Senses
© Patricia King 2014

Unless otherwise identified, Scripture quotations are taken from
the NEW AMERICAN STANDARD BIBLE®, Copyright
©1960,1962,1963,1968, 1971,1972,1973,1975,1977,1995 by
The Lockman Foundation. Used by permission. Some of the
verses are author's paraphrase.

Scripture quotations marked (KJV) are taken from the King
James Bible. Public domain.

Scripture quotations marked (NKJV) are taken from the New
King James Version®. Copyright © 1982 by Thomas Nelson,
Inc. Used by permission. All rights reserved.

Published and distributed by:

XP Publishing
XP Ministries
PO Box 1017
Maricopa AZ 85139
XPministries.com
All rights reserved. For Worldwide Distribution.

ISBN: 978-1-621661-48-1

TABLE OF CONTENTS

FOREWORD

James W. Goll

In this life, on occasion God grants you to walk alongside a champion – brave heart – general – trail blazer – pioneer. I have had such an honor these last several years in walking with one of this generation's leaders in the Body of Christ who loves well and has grit to fight!

Yes, you know who I am talking about. It is none other than the author of this new and needed forerunner book, *Developing Your Five Spiritual Senses* – my dear friend Patricia King.

I have roamed the nations in righteousness with this lady and have befriended her dear husband Ron. There are few people I have had the honor of walking with in this life who embrace the cross of Jesus more than this warrior bride!

Yes, I am one of her advisers; I pray for Patricia and Ron as well as XP Ministries and their team. And I have

7

bestowed upon this valiant woman the honor of leading and stewarding the ministry that my late wife Michal Ann and I started 18 years ago – "Women on the Frontlines." Wow, as soon as I passed the baton on to this "breaker," it grew overnight into a global movement! Jesus! Giving really works!

"So," you say, "I thought I was going to read another boring foreword to a book that James Goll put his stamp on." No! I am cheerleading for a friend; I am shouting from the rooftop. There are few in this Kingdom who never stop hungering for God and who bring forth treasures once lost in the dusty pages of church history, dust them off and attempt, in part, to bring them forth as shining lights of truth once again.

What do I get out of this? Joy and tears! Yes, I get the honor of opening the door to another jewel for the treasure chest of God! Does it get any better than this?

With deep appreciation, I am honored to open the door to yet another attempt to describe the indescribable: *Developing Your Five Spiritual Senses* by Patricia King.

Glory!

Dr. James W. Goll
Encounters Network • Prayer Storm • Compassion Acts
Author of *The Lifestyle of a Prophet, The Seer, Praying for Israel's Destiny* and scores of others

INTRODUCTION

In December 2001, I was granted a 30-day visitation in the Holy Spirit. During this visitation, the Lord daily revealed exciting biblical truth regarding the believer's God-given access into an encounter with Him and His invisible Kingdom realm. Since that time, I have been teaching what He revealed to me through our ministry's signature course: *The Glory School.*

So often in our western Christianity, we offer academic mental consent to parts of the Word of God that resonate with our world view in a practical sense, while we dismiss the parts of the Bible that disclose the believer's spiritual empowerment. Rather, should we not be fully embracing with authentic faith the spiritual truths, experiences, and invitations for supernatural encounter that we so clearly see communicated and proclaimed in the Holy Scriptures? By denying the spiritual aspects and supernatural activities of the Kingdom, we are in danger of falling into what Paul warned Timothy about:

> But realize this, that in the last days … men will be … holding to a form of godliness, although they have denied its power; avoid such men as these.
>
> **2 Timothy 3:1-5**

We should be naturally supernatural. The invisible realms of the Kingdom should be familiar to every believer. In this season, the Body of Christ is being awakened with a fresh hunger to live the Kingdom life as Jesus modeled it, with miracles, signs, wonders, visitations, and operations in the Spirit. Everywhere I go, I see this hunger in both believers and non-believers.

The Bible reveals five spiritual senses that believers can operate in – if you are a believer, that includes you! This book will acquaint you with those five God-given spiritual senses, defining and examining each one specifically. As you read, you will discover how to discern the function of each sense and how to develop and mature in the use and operation of each one. You will receive keys to understanding and tools for developing, utilizing, and maturing these very senses in your life.

Once we develop our spiritual senses, our personal relationship with the Lord will be enhanced. Intimacy with Him will increase ... and partnership with Him will be heightened. These are experiences that every believer is hungry for, and that is why YOU are interested in this book.

Enjoy the journey into the glorious discovery of your five spiritual senses.

We should be naturally supernatural. The invisible realms of the Kingdom should be familiar to every believer.

CHAPTER ONE

YOUR FIVE SPIRITUAL SENSES

God created you with five spiritual senses that parallel your five natural senses. You actually have these senses in you right now even though they might not be developed. Perhaps you are not even aware of them.

YOU ARE A SPIRITUAL BEING WITH SPIRITUAL SENSES.

Once you give your life to Christ, you are no longer a natural, earthly being attempting to get into heaven. You are not someone who struggles through life on earth hoping one day to escape the oppression in this earthly realm. Absolutely not!

Rather, in Christ you have become a heavenly being who lives on earth but whose citizenship is in heaven.

> So then you are no longer strangers and aliens, but you are fellow citizens with the saints, and are of God's household.
>
> **Ephesians 2:19**

You are a new creation; old things have passed away while all things have become new.

> Therefore if anyone is in Christ, he is a new creature; the old things passed away; behold, new things have come.
>
> **2 Corinthians 5:17**

You are seated in heavenly places in Christ, at the right hand of the Father.

> Which He brought about in Christ, when He raised Him from the dead and seated Him at His right hand in the heavenly places.
>
> **Ephesians 1:20**

> And raised us up with Him, and seated us with Him in the heavenly places in Christ Jesus.
>
> **Ephesians 2:6**

You are crucified with Christ, and His life now lives in you and through you.

> I have been crucified with Christ; and it is no longer
> I who live, but Christ lives in me; and the life which
> I now live in the flesh I live by the faith in the Son
> of God, who loved me and gave Himself up for me.
> **Galatians 2:20**

You have been stationed on earth by God as a heavenly ambassador, representing His Kingdom and reconciling man to God through the power of the Spirit.

> Therefore, we are ambassadors for Christ.
> **2 Corinthians 5:20**

As Christ is, so are you in this world, and the works that He did you will do also.

> So Jesus said to them again, "Peace be with you; as
> the Father has sent Me, I also send you."
> **John 20:21**

> Truly, truly I say to you, he who believes in Me, the
> works that I do, he will do also; and greater works
> than these will he do; because I go to the Father.
> **John 14:12**

Your life in Christ, your position in Christ, and your ministry in Christ is accomplished through the grace of our Lord Jesus and the empowerment of His most Holy Spirit.

> For by grace you have been saved through faith;
> and that not of yourselves, it is the gift of God; not
> as a result of works, so that no one may boast.
>
> **Ephesians 2:8-9**

God's grace is at work within you to accomplish His purposes in and through you while you journey in this earthly realm.

> For it is God who is at work in you, both to will and
> to work for His good pleasure.
>
> **Philippians 2:13**

When you live with this perspective, you will no longer struggle with failing self-effort to achieve a salvation that you believe will only fully manifest after your life on earth is over. Instead, your life will take on new meaning and the manifestation of a glorious Kingdom life will flow through you while you live on earth.

In Christ, You ARE a heavenly being living on earth (living in a physical body). You are no longer an earthly being struggling to make it to heaven.

As a heavenly being, you have five spiritual senses that acquaint you with the invisible realm of His Kingdom.

Bilocation

Bilocation means to live in two locations at the same time. You are living on earth, so you are familiar with and function in the earthly dimension through your physical life and five physical senses. But when you are in Christ, you are also a spiritual being with a born-again spirit that has five spiritual senses; you are familiar with and function in the unseen dimension of the Kingdom of God.

You can actually function in two realms at the same time. Jesus did! He explained this to Nicodemus:

> No one has ascended to heaven but He who came down from heaven, that is, the Son of Man who is in heaven.
> **John 3:13 NKJV**

Using this Scripture as a reference, we see that Jesus was standing on earth when He made this statement to Nicodemus, yet He was explaining that He was also in heaven as He was speaking to him.

As already stated, the Scriptures teach that you are seated in heavenly places in Christ (Ephesians 2:6) and yet, you are here living in the natural earth. Well, which one is it? Are you here or there? The answer is that you are in both places simultaneously. Your physical body relates to the earthly dimension and your spirit relates to the heavenly or spiritual dimension.

17

We discover through Scripture that we are a three-part being: spirit, soul, and body.

Now may the God of peace Himself sanctify you entirely; and may your spirit and soul and body be preserved complete, without blame at the coming of our Lord Jesus Christ.

1 Thessalonians 5:23

Your body relates to the physical dimension, your soul (mind, will, emotions) relates to the relational dimension, and your spirit relates to the spiritual dimension. All three parts of you have unique functions and can operate independently from each other at the same time. For example, my physical body can be washing dishes. I have washed dishes for many years and I do not need to engage my mind in this task; believe me, to this day, I can go into autopilot mode when I perform this task – smile.

However, at the same time my body is washing dishes, my mind (a faculty of the soul) can be totally uninvolved in my dishwashing, and perhaps is thinking about planning a dinner party later in the week. While my physical body is engaged in washing dishes and my soul is involved in planning a dinner party, I am praying in tongues in my spirit. (The Scripture teaches that when I pray in tongues, "my spirit prays.")

For if I pray in a tongue, my spirit prays, but my mind
is unfruitful.
1 Corinthians 14:14

Therefore, in this example, all three parts of me are functioning independently of each other – all at the same time.

Each part of you (your body, soul, and spirit), have the ability to "sense." For example, your physical body can sense physical pain. Your soul can sense fear. Your spirit can sense the presence of the Lord. You were created with the ability to sense.

Even though, as mentioned previously, our focus in this book is to reveal our five *spiritual* senses, it is interesting that the spiritual senses parallel the physical senses. The physical senses, however, relate to the physical realm and the spiritual senses relate to the spiritual.

Your will (part of the soul's function) determines the action you desire to take in response to what you sense. Your spiritual senses, as you will discover later in this book, can be developed and you can increase in spiritual awareness and effectiveness as a result. Most Christians are very aware of their physical senses but not so aware of their spiritual senses.

YOUR FIVE PHYSICAL SENSES

Your physical body has senses that function in and relate to the physical realm. Your five physical senses are:

HEARING

With this sense you have the ability to hear physical sounds, pitches, rhythms and words.

SEEING

This sense enables you to see physical substance such as print on a page, nature, light, physical activity and movement.

TASTING

God gave you the ability to taste distinct flavors through the taste buds on your tongue. When a substance is placed on your taste buds, you are able to detect its taste. You can also detect if its tasteless.

SMELLING

You have the physical ability to detect physical presence through smell. For example, if you walk into a house and smell fresh warm bread, what does that tell you? Possibly that there is bread in the oven and that you might just stick around for a taste?

Touching

God created nerve endings on your body so that you can be aware of the world around you. For example, if you close your eyes and run your hand over a velvet pillow, you can detect what it is. You can't see it, you can't smell it, you can't hear it, you can't taste it but you can feel it through touch.

The Soul's Response to Your Physical Senses

As mentioned earlier, when your body experiences something through the five physical senses, your soul (mind, will, emotions) becomes aware and makes decisions as a result. For example, you might walk down the street and smell pizza. You in your mind (soul) become aware of this and make a decision to buy a piece of pizza. After all, you are hungry and it smells good to you.

Another example is, if you put your hand close to a hot element, you will feel the heat and your mind will register the danger. As a result, you choose to pull your hand away. Your soul, which hosts your will, responds to the five physical senses.

Developing Your Senses

If you were to walk around blindfolded, it would not take long to realize that your other four senses greatly increased in sensitivity and perception. I was with a friend in Ottawa, Canada, a while ago and he shared about a restaurant in their city that is very unique. All the workers are blind. There is no light in the restaurant and when clients come in they are escorted to their seats in the dark. Someone tells them what's on the menu. They cannot see anything – not even the food when it comes. This restaurant has become very popular because of the unique experience it offers.

Customers testify that the taste and texture of the food is enhanced and they are more aware of their environment, including the sounds and smells in the room. They have to feel for their napkins, cutlery, and plate. They take their time eating, as they taste and feel the texture of the food. They hear sounds in the room that they never noticed before. They become more aware of the people they are with, as they need to focus more on their presence and sense where they are sitting and what they are doing.

I was intrigued and wondered if such a restaurant would have many customers, but apparently it is so popular that there are many more restaurants springing up.

In military training, soldiers are trained to enhance their senses so that in times of war and attack they will be alert and aware. They practice specific sense-enhancing exercises for this very purpose.

You can enhance your natural senses through exercise and focus. The Bible says that you can also train your spiritual senses by reason of practice.

> But solid food is for the mature, who because of practice have their senses trained to discern good and evil.
>
> **Hebrews 5:14**

YOUR FIVE SPIRITUAL SENSES

Your five spiritual senses parallel your natural senses. Below is a brief explanation of each sense.

HEARING

With this spiritual sense you are able to identify and discern the voice and sounds of God, angels, demonic spirits, and the sounds of activities in the spiritual realm.

SEEING

This spiritual sense enables you to see and discern substance, beings, and activity in the unseen dimension.

TASTING

Even as you have a physical sense that enables you to taste things in the physical realm, you also have "spiritual taste buds." The spiritual world contains substances you can taste.

SMELLING

There are fragrances and odors in the spiritual world, and God has created in you the ability to detect and identify them.

TOUCHING

You are able to feel and discern things spiritually with this sense.

The following chapters provide you with greater revelation and understanding on the development of each of your five spiritual senses.

PRAYER

If you desire to develop your five spiritual senses, pray this prayer:

> Dear Heavenly Father,
>
> I believe that You created me with a spirit, soul, and body and that You have given me five spiritual senses in order for me to draw close to You and to become more aware of Your Kingdom realm. I pray, in the name of Jesus, for my spiritual senses to be opened and to develop in heightened discernment and function. Lead me by Your Spirit into this marvelous discovery and growth.
>
> Thank You, Father!

CHAPTER TWO

THE SPIRITUAL SENSE OF HEARING

Jesus said: My sheep hear My voice, and I know them, and they follow Me.

John 10:27

Hearing God is so important to our relationship with Him, for how can you enjoy relationship with someone you cannot communicate with? When we hear God we draw close to Him; we can then follow and obey Him.

I remember as a new Christian learning to identify the voice of God. Most of the time I heard Him while I was praying or reading my Bible. I had been a Christian for only a few days when I read Isaiah 60 and 61. At that moment, it was as if I was no longer reading the Scriptures but rather it was God speaking to me personally through the Scriptures. It was all so real and so personal. To this day (almost 40 years later) those verses are still a personal word to me. Many such verses have become spiritual reality in my life. God spoke and I heard.

I remember sitting in my prayer chair about ten and a half months into my salvation journey. I was discouraged because I had been saved for nearly eleven months yet my husband still had not come to the Lord. I was actually complaining about it, murmuring before the Lord, "Isn't Ron ever going to get saved?"

To my surprise, He answered back. I had not even been expecting an answer but it was there loud and clear in my thoughts. He said, "Yes, he will." I was elated and asked Him a further question, this time seriously engaged as I waited for His answer. I asked, "When?" The answer came back immediately, but it was not the answer I expected. I thought He would tell me how many days, weeks or months it would be, but instead He said, "As soon as you release your control over your husband and let Me accomplish his entrance into My Kingdom."

Wow, that stung! But I knew the conviction was right on. I had tried so hard to set up all the right meetings for Ron to connect with pastors and mature Christians.

My attempts failed terribly and only served to harden his heart more toward the Lord. That day, because I heard the voice of God, everything changed. I repented, and within a week my husband came to the Lord. In fact, I was given the blessing by God to lead Ron to Christ in prayer.

Oh, I am so glad we can hear the voice of God! It is different from any other voice. It is powerful and life-changing! His voice produces miracles and imparts grace.

The voice of the Lord is upon the waters;

The God of glory thunders,

The Lord is over many waters.

The voice of the Lord is powerful,

The voice of the Lord is majestic.

The voice of the Lord breaks the cedars;

Yes, the Lord breaks in pieces the cedars of Lebanon.

He makes Lebanon skip like a calf,

And Sirion like a young wild ox.

The voice of the Lord hews out flames of fire.

The voice of the Lord shakes the wilderness;

The Lord shakes the wilderness of Kadesh.

The voice of the Lord makes the deer to calve and strips the forests bare;

And in His temple everything says, "Glory."

Psalm 29:3-9

Three Sources

Many people ask, "How do I know that I am hearing from God and not from myself?" This is a good question, since we hear from three main sources.

1. God

God speaks to people. All through the Bible you see God communicating with mankind. When He speaks, His words and message always align with His character, nature, and Word. That is how you can discern if you are hearing from Him. For example, His nature is righteous and pure, so He will never speak to you in corrupt or immoral ways. His words will always be supported by Scripture. It is easy to test in that sense.

2. Self

Another source is your own natural self. The Bible says that the carnal nature (the flesh) of man is contrary to the Spirit of God.

When God speaks, His words and messages always align with His character, nature and Word. He is righteous and pure and will never speak to you in corrupt ways. His words will always be supported by Scripture.

> Because the carnal mind is enmity against God: for it is not subject to the law of God, neither indeed can be.
>
> **Romans 8:7 KJV**

When I desire to hear from God, I do not want my own agendas, thoughts, imaginations, etc., in the way. The Bible says that I can literally cast down thoughts from my own mind so they will not interfere with hearing from God.

> Casting down imaginations, and every high thing that exalts itself against the knowledge of God, and bringing into captivity every thought to the obedience of Christ.
>
> **2 Corinthians 10:5 KJV**

Before I seek the Lord, I pray a simple prayer to eliminate my "self" as an option when attempting to hear from God: "In Jesus' name, I cast down every thought, imagination, and agenda that is sourced in my own carnal nature. I only submit myself to hearing from the Holy Spirit."

3. THE DEVIL

The devil (and his demonic cohorts) tempts us. Therefore he has a voice. The Scripture says that he is the father of lies (John 8:44), so we do not want to submit to him or listen to what he has to say. I like to eliminate his voice when seeking the Lord by praying:

> "In the name of Jesus, I bind all demonic interference and forbid him to speak to me."

In Matthew 16:19, Jesus said that whatever we "bind" on earth will be backed up by heaven. To *bind* means to tie up as with chains, to muzzle, to keep from straying or operating.

If we cast down our own thoughts, imaginations, and agendas, bind the enemy, and then invite the Holy Spirit to fill us afresh as we listen for God's voice, we will grow in our ability to hear the voice of God.

Some Ways to Hear with Your Spiritual Sense of Hearing

1. "God-thoughts"

The most common way people hear spiritually is in their thoughts. Again, the important thing to consider here is the source. Your mind can host thoughts from the three different sources we mentioned earlier, but our greatest desire is to grow in our discernment and our ability to identify those thoughts that come from God. These thoughts will most often come in the same way that you receive other thoughts, but their source is God. You can identify them by testing them to see if they line up with His character, nature, and Word.

When I was a young minister, I was asked to preach at a Sunday morning service in a local church. I prayed and sought the Lord for over a month but I could not get a message. To be honest, I entered into an anxious state. The night before I was scheduled to preach I still had not received the message. I had no notes, no inspiration, no nothing! I attempted to wake my husband up to have him share the worry-party with me, but it was a "no go." He simply said, "Go to sleep. You will get the message in time." I thought, 'That's fine for him to say, he doesn't have to preach." I started to imagine what it would look like if I stood on the platform with no message and then … I worried some more.

When the morning sun started to rise, I still did not have my message. Full of anxiety, tears, and apprehension, I got up and went for a drive to a lake near the place where we were staying. Getting out of the car, I sat on the edge of the lake pleading with God for a message … but still nothing. I looked out over the water and saw my reflection in it. Then the still, small, inner voice of God spoke clearly and gently in my thoughts: "Share reflections of your life. Open your mouth and I will fill it."

The entrance of the word brings light and creates faith. That one simple little God-thought changed everything for me. I knew what to do now and I could trust Him to work it all out.

The church came unglued that day as I ministered, and many people were deeply touched. A considerable number came to Jesus. The altar was full.

Another time, I heard the Lord speak to me through the memory of an incident that happened years ago while I was working at my office in a commercial building. On this day, a man came through the door, introduced himself and began to ask me questions about our ministry (he had seen the sign on the door stating that we were a Christian ministry). He desired to sell me a product and business plan he was featuring, and in the conversation he said, "I am a Christian, too." I was excited to hear that and was going to continue on in conversation when an inner voice (thought) came into my mind that said, "No, he is not a Christian. – he is lying." It was such a strong thought! And seemingly out of nowhere. It made me cautious. I asked him to share how he came to Jesus, and the entire time I listened to him, the voice in my thoughts said, "This is not true. He is making it up."

I politely asked him to leave even though he was very aggressive and persistent in his sales pitch. I discovered later that he was involved in a deceptive marketing plan and had deceived many. The voice of God protected me.

When the voice of the Lord speaks in revelation like that, there is no condemnation. Rather, He speaks it like a fact. I have never known the Lord's voice to be condemning or accusing, but it has certainly been revealing and sometimes strict.

2. AUDIBLE VOICES AND SOUNDS

Sometimes you can hear sounds that are audible to the natural ear but they are from the spiritual realm. You might hear a specific sound with your spiritual sense of hearing that others might not hear. I remember one time I was teaching a Glory School in Canada where over 80% of the class heard the sound of shofars (ram's horn trumpets). But there was not a shofar to be found in the natural. It was so clear that it seemed like someone was actually physically in the room blowing it.

Another time, I heard my name spoken audibly. And on one occasion, I heard God audibly speak a message to me. Other times I have heard alarms or telephones ringing which awakened me from sleep, but the alarm or the phone was not ringing in the physical realm. This has happened to me several times.

I often hear angels singing during worship. They sing on a higher pitch or realm than in the natural, so I can easily distinguish it. The very first time I heard angels singing, I had been a Christian for less than a year. It was as though I had earphones on. I could hear nothing else in the room, but my ears – my entire being, actually –

were full of the sound of a multitude of angels singing. It was like the sound of instruments singing.

3. INNER AUDIBLE VOICES

Sometimes your spiritual sense of hearing will identify an inner audible voice or sound. This is stronger and more defined than a thought, but it is not outside of the body. You hear this sound from within, and it sounds so strong and clear that it has the same impact as if it had come from outside.

A number of years ago when I was on the mission field, I was driving down a road and about to turn onto a street that led to my destination. As I was ready to make the turn, I heard an inner audible voice say, "Do NOT turn onto that street." It was so strong that I kept going. I discovered later that gang members had shot someone at a home on that street around the time I'd have turned onto it; they actually killed two people. That inner voice saved me from being in the midst of a dangerous situation.

Sometimes your spiritual sense of hearing will identify an inner audible voice or sound. Though you hear it within, it sounds so strong and clear that it has the same impact as if it had come from outside.

Another time (again on the mission field) I was tired and wanted to go back to the hotel. It had been a long day of ministry in the midst of the rainy season in Cambodia. We had been walking through mud all day and I felt worn-out, hungry, and in need of a shower. I just wanted to go back to my room, get cleaned up, eat some pizza, and go to bed – and that is exactly where I was headed, until an inner audible voice said, "Will you go with Me to one more location? I have an assignment for you there."

It was stronger than a thought in my mind. It was "The Voice." Immediately I knew that the shower, pizza, and bed were going to have to wait. We followed the Lord's leading to that location and were privileged to aid in the rescue of a child who was a sex slave. This child has been in our care and legal custody ever since. His life was radically changed by "The Voice."

4. DREAMS

Dreams are often played out like a movie. You can detect both motion and sound. You can hear the sounds of water, wind, voices, instruments and noise in your dreams. Not all dreams are spiritual but many of them are, and they contain messages. You know that a spiritual dream is different, as it is more impacting than a normal dream and it leaves you in remembrance of it.

I remember one time hearing sounds in my dream that had significant impact on my life. I was believing for funds to go on a ministry assignment. It was my last day to purchase the airfare and as of yet the funds had not manifested. Before I woke up on the final morning to purchase the fare, I had a dream in which I saw a stack of $20 bills that totaled the entire amount I needed, followed by an audible voice in the dream that said emphatically, "Go buy your ticket."

Throughout that morning, God supernaturally provided all the fare to me in $20 bills. By the afternoon, I was able to go to the travel agent and purchase the ticket.

5. Visual Messages

Have you ever driven down a road and a billboard that you have passed dozens of times before suddenly stands out to you, and you are immediately impacted by a message through it in a way that has nothing to do with its original statement or meaning? Is it as if God is speaking to you profoundly through the billboard? That is because He probably is. The same can happen with other signs or license plate numbers, labels, or quotes in a book. You can hear a message through the understanding that comes to you through these visual triggers.

Two of our team members were traveling back from Tucson to our base in Maricopa, Arizona. They stopped at Casa Grande for gasoline, then got back on the highway with about 20–30 minutes before their turnoff. Immediately, they both saw a flash of light out of their peripheral vision. Hardly an instant later, they noticed that they had gone past the turnoff to Maricopa. They were shocked and looked at each other in amazement, as this was impossible in the natural. One asked the other, "Did we just get transported in the Spirit?" They both thought that this could be a possibility but asked God for a confirmation. Suddenly a transport truck pulled in front of them. The signage of the company was written across the back of the truck: "Covenant Transport." They knew they had heard the voice of confirmation from the Lord.

The Lord often will speak to me in numbers. For a long season I was seeing 818 and 111 everywhere – on clocks, timers, license plates, channels, etc. God was speaking a confirmation to Scripture portions He had given me in my devotion times: Deuteronomy 8:18 and 1:11. Every time I saw those numbers I was reminded of the promises in those verses.

6. ANGELS

Sometimes God sends angels to bring messages to His people. When they showed up in the Bible, they often said such things as "Fear not," or in the case of Mary, mother of Jesus, Gabriel said, "Hail, favored one." It is not unusual for angels to bring messages today. Sometimes you cannot see the angels but you can hear them.

While traveling across Canada, I had an angelic encounter. In that experience the voice of the Lord spoke through an angel, declaring that He was watching over His Word to perform it over our nation.

In my first third-heaven visitation in 1994, I heard masses of angelic voices laughing. The Lord reminded me of Psalm 2:4, "He who sits in the heavens laughs."

TESTING WHAT YOU HEAR

Everything needs to be tested and the source discerned. As I mentioned earlier, you can discern the voice of God. His voice is loving, kind, truthful, and full of grace, righteousness, and purity. His voice always conforms to His character, His nature and His Word – these are your three measuring tools.

The voice of the flesh and the demonic can be accusatory, condemning, selfish, greedy, contrary to

Scripture, and contrary to the nature and Word of God. God's voice, however, is loving, full of truth, mercy, righteousness, and pure – always confirmed by the Scriptures.

You also want to test the content in the light of its importance in your life. Why are you receiving this information? What is its purpose in your life? How do you apply it?

There are three stages to revelation:

1. Receiving the revelation.

2. Interpreting the revelation.

3. Applying the revelation.

Prayfully discern each of these stages for accuracy. When you receive a revelation, pray, test it, and discern its source. Then pray that you will be able to discern the correct interpretation. After receiving the interpretation, pray that you may discern how to apply it correctly. Remember: God often speaks in "parables" rather than in "plain speech." He also may use symbolism.

Perhaps you are to spend time in prayer for what He revealed to you. Or ponder the things in your heart for a while. Or there may be immediate specific action that you need to take. Discern how to apply it. And be a good steward of what you hear from Him.

PREPARING TO HEAR

When preparing to hear:

1. GET RID OF UNWANTED OPTIONS

As mentioned before, you can eliminate the options of the carnal flesh and the demonic by praying a prayer to cast down your own thoughts, imaginations, burdens and perceptions and to bind the devil's voice in Jesus' name. When you pray this prayer of preparation in faith, without doubting, you are positioning yourself to eliminate those options.

HERE IS A SAMPLE PRAYER:

In the name of Jesus, I cast down my own carnal thoughts, imaginations, perceptions, and burdens that rise up against the knowledge of God. I also, in Jesus' name, bind any demonic voice, sound, agenda or temptation that will taint my spiritual ability to hear accurately from God. AMEN.

2. SANCTIFY YOURSELF

Sanctification means to set yourself apart for God. Your mind, for example, was created by God for you to reason with Him and to receive His thoughts. Because of the fall of mankind, we have allowed sinful thoughts in our mind. It is possible to have pure water flowing from a pure source, but if it goes through rusty pipes it gets contaminated. You want to hear accurately, so invite the Holy Spirit to convict you of any unconfessed sin and then ask Him to forgive you for any thoughts that have entered your mind that were not of Him. He will forgive you and cleanse your mind from all unrighteousness (1 John 1:9).

3. BE FILLED AFRESH WITH THE HOLY SPIRIT

I also like to invite the Holy Spirit to fill me afresh with His life, His light, and His love when I am seeking to hear His voice. When you are filled completely with the Holy Spirit, you can be assured you will hear from Him.

You receive by faith the holy confidence that you will hear from God, as (1) you believe that God answered your prayer to lay down the unwanted options, (2) you set yourself apart for God, and (3) you believe that you are filled afresh with the Holy Spirit.

4. LISTEN

You can hear if you are listening. Listen for the voice of the Holy Spirit and you will grow in the discernment.

HOW TO DEVELOP YOUR ABILITY TO HEAR

The following are some helpful points to aid you in developing your hearing ability in the spirit.

1. POSTURE YOURSELF TO LISTEN

Mary at Bethany postured herself at the feet of Jesus and hung on every word He spoke, while Martha was distracted with many preparations (Luke 10:38-42). I have discovered that the more I posture myself to listen for His voice, the more I hear. In 1 Samuel 3:9, young Samuel said, "Speak, Lord, for Your servant is listening."

Have you ever had someone say to you, "Shhh, do you hear that?" You answered, "No, I don't hear anything." They replied, "Shhh… listen!" Then, as you quieted your thoughts and concentrated on listening, you heard.

This works the same way in developing your spiritual sense of hearing.

2. READ THE WORD, LOOKING FOR THE RHEMA

The Scriptures are inspired by Holy Spirit. In other words they are authored by God. As you read the Word, ask the Lord to "speak to you." Jesus said, "The words that I speak to you are spirit, and they are life" (John 6:63 NKJV). If you just read through the Bible academically, you will receive a blessing, but when you read to "hear what the Spirit is saying," you will receive what is called "rhema." This is a Greek word referring to the Spirit-quickened word. This is your fresh bread from heaven.

Try reading through the Bible until a particular portion "jumps out at you." That is God speaking. You are hearing what the Spirit is speaking to you. The more you seek for rhema (Spirit-quickened Word), the more you will find it. The more you read the Word, the more opportunity there is for the Spirit to speak to you.

3. JOURNAL

I find journaling (writing down in a diary what I am hearing) very powerful. Journal what you believe you are hearing from God. Then go over it again and again, meditating on it, pondering it. Let it go deep into your heart and become part of you. I also find it beneficial to go back over old journals and read through revelations the Spirit gave in the past. Sometimes He will re-engage with you regarding those revelations and build them deeper and stronger.

4. ASK QUESTIONS THAT DEMAND AN ANSWER

One helpful way I have found to develop my ability to hear is to deliberately ask God a question that needs an answer. For example, inquire of Him concerning a situation that you need wisdom for, and then wait on

Him for an answer. Journal your question, listen for His response and then journal His response. Sometimes He will lead you to a number of Scriptures that have keys in them, or He may speak to you in faint God-thoughts. At other times, over the next few days or weeks you will find Him speaking to you through unexpected circumstances or "God-moments."

5. CONFIRM WITH THE WORD

Develop your ability to hear by confirming everything with the Scriptures. Prophet Bob Jones, before he went to glory, would always say, "Check out all your spiritual encounters with the Scriptures." By committing to this process, you will develop maturity, accuracy, and excellence in your ability to hear.

6. BELIEVE (FAITH AND ACTION)

Faith is vital in everything to do with Kingdom life. Believe first of all that you CAN hear from God and then believe in what you have received. The children of Israel heard the voice of God but they doubted and hardened their hearts afterward. Our walk with God is a walk of faith. He wants us to believe. Do not be afraid to take a risk. Act in faith.

The Lord gave me this funny scenario one time regarding hearing the Lord's voice and acting on it. There was a man who desperately wanted to hear from God. As he was listening, he thought God said, "Get rid of your garage." Wanting to respond in faith and obedience, he immediately went out to his yard and tore down his garage. It was in need of repair anyway. The Lord was watching him and suddenly called all His angels, the great cloud of witnesses, and other heavenly beings to observe this act of faith and obedience. As the heavenly hosts watched, God explained, "He thought I said, 'Get rid of your garage,' but I actually said, 'Get rid of your grudge.'"

Obviously he had not yet quite hit the mark on hearing accurately, but God was impressed with his faith. This young man had believed and he acted on what he believed he heard.

You will develop as much through your mistakes as through your successes. You will become seasoned in hearing as you exercise your senses. Believe and act.

Don't be afraid to step out and believe what you are hearing. At times you might not get it all perfect, but God is cheering you on for trying. When my grandson started walking, his first steps weren't perfect; in fact, he would take one or two steps and then fall. He was not steady on his feet yet, but that is how children learn to walk. It is a normal process. It would be so sad to see a child stay in the crib until becoming a twenty-year-old because of the fear of not being able to walk perfectly, even though trying. Having a few falls is all part of the process.

I am so glad you are walking!

But without faith it is impossible to please Him, for he who comes to God must believe that He is, and that He is a rewarder of those who diligently seek Him.

Hebrews 11:6 NKJV

CHAPTER THREE

THE SPIRITUAL
SENSE OF SEEING

The Bible offers several references to seeing in the realm of the spirit. One significant example is in 2 Kings 6:14-17 where Elisha was surrounded by a great army. He was not concerned because he could see beyond the natural realm into the spirit realm. He saw that there were more with him than against him. Seeing this gave him great confidence, courage, and faith.

Elisha's servant could not see into this realm. He was fearful and despairing. Elisha prayed to God that his servant's eyes would open to see into the invisible realm. As a result, this servant was given spiritual vision enabling him to see the armies of God that were there to defend them.

> And Elisha prayed, and said, Lord, I pray thee, open his eyes, that he may see. And the Lord opened the eyes of the young man; and he saw: and, behold, the mountain was full of horses and chariots of fire round about Elisha.
>
> **2 Kings 6:17 KJV**

The apostle Paul understood the importance of spiritual vision and prayed specifically for the church at Ephesus to have their eyes open. Many believers continue to pray this prayer today:

> That the God of our Lord Jesus Christ, the Father of glory, may give to you the spirit of wisdom and revelation in the knowledge of Him, the eyes of your understanding being enlightened; that you may know what is the hope of His calling, what are the riches of the glory of His inheritance in the saints.
>
> **Ephesians 1:17-18 KJV**

THE SPIRITUAL SENSE OF SEEING ENABLES YOU TO:

1. SPIRITUALLY PERCEIVE (EYES OF UNDERSTANDING)

- The ability to see, hear, or become aware of something through spiritual revelation.
- The state of being or process of becoming aware of something through the spiritual senses.

- A way of regarding, understanding, or interpreting something by the Spirit; a mental impression.

And Jesus, aware of this, said to them, "Why do you discuss the fact that you have no bread? Do you not yet see or understand? Do you have a hardened heart? Having eyes, do you not see?

Mark 8:17-18

This type of perception gives you the ability to "see truth" – to have your spiritual eyes open to understand the ways of the Spirit. I can often see the lights go on in people's hearts when they see the truth. You can probably remember times when your spiritual eyes (perception and understanding) were opened to behold truth from the Lord. It is glorious. Before reading the Word, ask for the eyes of your understanding to be opened so that you can receive revelation from the Lord.

2. To See Images, Beings, and Motion in the Spiritual Realm

The word of the Lord came to me saying, "What do you see, Jeremiah?" And I said, "**I see** a rod of an almond tree."

Jeremiah 1:11

And the angel came in unto her and said, Hail, thou that art highly favoured, the Lord is with thee: blessed art thou among women. And **when she**

saw him, she was troubled at his saying, and cast in her mind what manner of salutation this should be.

Luke 1:28-29 KJV

And it shall come to pass in the last days, saith God, I will pour out of my Spirit upon all flesh: and your sons and your daughters shall prophesy, and your young men shall **see visions**, and your old men shall dream dreams.

Acts 2:17 KJV

The Bible is full of examples in which God's people saw a vision with their spiritual sense of seeing. Ezekiel saw the cherubim in Ezekiel 10 and the valley of dry bones in Ezekiel 37. Daniel and John saw end time visions. Many others in the Bible recorded the vision they saw. As a believer in Jesus, you have the ability to see in the spirit, too.

SOME WAYS YOU CAN SEE WITH YOUR SPIRITUAL SENSE OF SEEING:

1. FAINT IMAGES AND IMPRESSIONS IN THE MIND OR IMAGINATION

The most common way believers see is by identifying images that God puts in their imagination. Sometimes these are very faint. We need to learn to pay attention to these powerful images. Your imagination is that part of your mind that God created in you to receive vision and images. You will always "see" through the use of the imagination. You will never, for example, have a vision in your big toe, your lips, lungs, or liver. No, vision is always connected to your imagination. Once you have a vision, you can recall it, as it is imbedded in the imagination's memory bank.

Many are afraid that what they are receiving is "just their imagination" – but don't discount this wonderful means God has given you to see images. We need to celebrate the imagination and embrace the things God reveals to us through its use. The question would be, "What is the source of what we are seeing?" We are seeking God's inspiration and vision.

I was praying for a woman once in a prayer line. I did not know what she was in line for, but when I laid my hands on her I saw an impression in my mind's eye of a baby in her womb. It was not a really vivid impression but I felt to move on it. I had a sense that I was to break

Don't be afraid of receiving something "just in your imagination," which is a wonderful means God has given you to see images. Rather ask, "What is the source of what we are seeing?" We are seeking God's inspiration and vision.

barrenness off her and declare fertility. I did so and she screamed, "I have always wanted a child, but I am barren!" I responded with faith and excitement, saying, "I see a baby in your womb. I believe that you will become pregnant." Sure enough, two months later she called me and told me she was pregnant. She gave birth to that baby and had two more babies after that.

Do not underestimate even the faintest of visions.

2. Open vision

An open vision is when you are actually seeing into the spirit realm with your physical eyes open. Your spiritual sense of "seeing" and your natural sense become synchronized in this type of vision. Sometimes an individual might see something but no one else in the room does.

One night I was in my living room praying with some friends. Our living room had an open-vaulted ceiling that was at least sixteen feet high with a dining room on the upper level that you could see from the living room below. I looked up from my prayers and saw with open vision a large angel that filled the room, with the top of its head going through the roof. The angel was over twenty feet tall. I saw its form, its color, and some of its features. Totally taken aback, I screamed, as I did not expect to see it. There were others in the room that night but I was the only one who saw the angel. When I screamed, it disappeared from my vision and I have never seen that angel again with open vision. It is still so vivid to me. When I think of it, I once again can "see" it through my memory's eye. I have seen angels at other times, also, with open vision.

I also see lights and glory clouds at times with open vision. Sometimes they are flashes that I see out of my peripheral vision. On other occasions I have seen streams of light with various colors or a visible cloud that hovers over an area.

Oftentimes, people think that an open vision or trance carries more authority or is more powerful than a faint impression in the mind's eye. Although it is certainly more dramatic, it is not necessarily more powerful or authoritative. It is simply a different way that God uses to communicate. Each way is unique and each way is significant. It is the same with the still small thoughts in our mind versus the audible voice. They are simply different. One way is not more important than another.

One time the Lord asked me, "When did you have to raise your voice with your two sons as they were growing up?" I replied, "When they were far away or they weren't listening." The Lord explained to me that it is the same with Him and His relationship with us. The faint, either in vision or in sound, does not necessarily mean it is less important or less powerful.

3. CLOSED EYE VISION

In a closed eye vision your physical eyes are closed and yet you see a vivid, clear vision in your mind's eye, almost as clear as you would if your eyes were open. It is more precise and clear than a faint image or impression in the mind or imagination.

4. TRANCE VISION

A trance vision is when you find yourself in a dream-like state while you are awake. You are actually in the vision when in a trance. The vision is clean and vivid.

I was praying for a friend the very first time I went into a trance vision. Immediately I was in a realm where I saw immeasurable numbers of spiritual blessings floating in this realm. I realized by the Spirit that I was actually in Ephesians 1:3, which reads: "Blessed be the God and Father of our Lord Jesus Christ, who has blessed us with every spiritual blessing in the heavenly places in Christ." In that encounter, the Lord revealed action steps of faith for me to take in order to secure His will in a particular situation I had been praying for.

5. DREAM

When you are asleep you can dream. Sometimes, your dream will be spiritual in its source and you will "see" scenarios played out before you that have spiritual significance. The Bible has many examples of God or angels visiting in dreams with messages for the recipient. Bible characters like Joseph, Nebuchadnezzar, and others had dreams. Dreams are often revealed in symbolic form and require interpretation from God. If you ask for interpretation, He will reveal it to you.

I have experienced some profound dreams. Some have been impartation of revelation and insights, others have given me direction, and others have been warning dreams to keep me safe from harm.

6. DAYDREAM

In a daydream you are awake but you go into a dreamlike state. It is not as vivid or realistic as a trance, but in your mind a scenario is played out. Sometimes daydreams are initiated by God.

My call to preach was given to me in a daydream when I was a young Christian. When I first had this daydream, I did not understand that it was actually the Lord revealing my destiny. In fact, it came back three times, and each time I cast it down thinking it was my own mind initiating it. I thought I was in pride, so I kept repenting. It was a couple of years later when the exact daydream came to pass. The Lord spoke to me at that time saying, "This day is that daydream fulfilled."

PREPARING TO SEE

1. GET RID OF UNWANTED OPTIONS

Again, it is important to realize that we can see things from three different sources: God, self, or the devil. You will want to eliminate all sources that are not of God. Pray a prayer to cast down your own thoughts, imaginations, burdens and perceptions, binding the devil's visions in Jesus' name. When you pray this prayer of preparation in faith, without doubting, you are eliminating those options.

HERE IS A SAMPLE PRAYER:

In the name of Jesus, I cast down my own carnal thoughts, imaginations, perceptions, and burdens that are raised up against the knowledge of God. I also, in Jesus' name, bind any demonic vision, agenda, or temptation that will taint my spiritual vision. AMEN.

2. SANCTIFY YOUR IMAGINATION

Remember that sanctification means to set yourself apart for God. Your imagination was created by God so that you would be able to receive vision like He does. Originally, your imagination (vision center) was pure and untainted but because of the fall of mankind, sinful images have filled our imaginations. As mentioned earlier, pure water can only flow from a pure source; it gets contaminated if it has to go through rusty pipes. You want to see accurately, so invite the Holy Spirit to convict you of any unconfessed sin and then ask Him to forgive you for any images that have entered your imagination that were not of Him. He will forgive you and cleanse your mind from all unrighteousness (1 John 1:9).

3. BE FILLED AFRESH WITH THE HOLY SPIRIT

When your imagination is filled with the Holy Spirit, you are empowered to see with your spiritual sense of sight. Sometimes I like to soak in the presence of the Lord, intentionally inviting Him to fill my mind and imagination with His power and presence. I invite Him to awaken my vision to see as He sees.

4. LOOK

Have you ever noticed something as you were driving down the highway, then immediately said to your friends sitting in the back seat, "Wow, look at that!" You are

Soak in the Lord's presence, inviting Him to fill your mind and imagination with His power and presence. Invite Him to awaken your vision to see as He sees.

seeing something but they are not yet. They have to look in order to see what you are seeing.

Sometimes, like in a dream, you are not actually looking for a vision – the vision comes to you. However, you can also prepare yourself to see with your spiritual sense by intentionally "looking." In other words, be intentional about seeing. Look for what God might show you.

I have played the hide and seek game with my grandchildren. I hide little treasures and surprises for them (usually somewhere within their vision, depending on how old they are) so that they will find them. They then go looking for the treasures. When they look, they find.

This is how you can posture yourself to develop your spiritual sense of seeing. Look for vision with intentionality. You will be amazed at how you will become more seasoned in seeing if you simply look.

WAYS TO DEVELOP YOUR SENSE OF SEEING:

1. POSTURE OF EXPECTATION

Putting yourself in a position to see is always important. Take time in your schedule to meet with God in a place where there are no distractions. Pray through the preparation points mentioned above and wait on God with expectation. Believe that you are able to see and that you will see.

2. MEDITATION ON BIBLE VISIONS

One of the tools that will enhance your ability to see is to submit your mind and imagination to the visions found in Scripture. All Scripture has been inspired by the Holy Spirit, and the prophets in the Scripture communicated under powerful unction and anointing. When you meditate on these God-inspired portions and submit the visions within them to your imagination, you will open up your seer capacity.

Take a portion of Scripture such as Ezekiel 1 that is full of vision. Meditate on one verse at a time, inviting the Holy Spirit to reveal the vision and imprint it in your imagination. Let your imagination see what He showed the prophet. Let your mind's eye see it – or imagine it. The authority of the Word and vision you are meditating on, as revealed to you by the Spirit, will awaken your sense of seeing.

3. DRAW THE VISION

Another tool that has helped me is to draw the impressions the Lord reveals to me. It is fun to color the drawing also, according to how you see it in your mind's eye. You can use your devotional journal for this and then you have it to review later.

My friends bought me a paint easel, stand, paints, and canvas for my birthday one year. I'd close the door to my office, put on some worship music and invite the Holy Spirit to inspire vision within me. As He did, I would paint aspects of it on the canvas. It helped awaken the spiritual "seeing" sense.

4. THE POWER OF TESTIMONY

Another tool is to read about or listen to the God-inspired visions other believers have had. As you read the description of their vision or listen to them share it, ask the Holy Spirit to help you picture it in your mind's eye. Again, this is another awakening tool for your seeing sense.

You have been given eyes to see – both in the natural and in the spirit. May your spiritual vision be opened to behold the glories of Christ's love and Kingdom.

CHAPTER FOUR

THE SPIRITUAL SENSE OF TASTING

Most times, our spiritual senses are perceptions rather than a physical connection to the spiritual realm.

For example, you have probably heard people say, "That situation left a bad taste in my mouth." They are not suggesting that they experienced a physical taste but rather they had a negative encounter that left them with a "bad taste" – a perception or discernment.

> Is there iniquity in my tongue? Cannot my taste discern perverse things?
>
> **Job 6:30 KJV**

I am sure you have experienced a "bitter taste" after you heard someone speaking negative of another, or when you have walked into a room where there was coarse and perverse language. It left a "bad taste" in your mouth in regards to that environment.

In contrast, I am sure you can relate to this scenario: After a really good devotion time, church service, or conference – when you are filled with His presence and glory, you might come out of the meeting and think, "Wow, – that tasted good!" ... it was satisfying and fulfilling. You are tasting of the Lord and seeing that He is good.

Taste and see that the Lord is good.

Psalm 34:8

Joshua Mills was ministering in one of our meetings a number of years ago. As he was preparing in his hotel room, a supernatural phenomena took place: Oil started pouring out of his hands. Yes, real, tangible, Holy Spirit-produced oil! My husband, who was helping him get from his room to the meeting place, put a cup under Joshua's hands to catch the oil. By the time they reached the meeting room, the oil had filled half the cup. It continued to pour out of his hands and when he got up to speak, it started pouring out from his feet. He took his shoes off and we put an altar cloth and towel underneath to soak up the oil. It was awesome!

After he finished preaching, he prayed for everyone in the meeting and anointed them with the oil God gave. After the meeting he still had some oil left. I asked if I could taste it. When I put some on my tongue it had the taste of soap, and yet it smelled like wine. The Lord said that He was cleansing His people (soap) and healing them (wine).

God allowed me to literally taste His sign and wonder. This was a time when my physical sense of taste and my spiritual sense of taste converged. It was a wonderful experience for which I am truly grateful.

ACTIVATING YOUR SPIRITUAL SENSE OF TASTING

When you develop your spiritual sense of tasting, you are actually awakening your discernment of good and evil.

For example, the psalmist said:

How sweet are thy words unto my **taste**! Yea, sweeter than honey to my mouth!
Psalm 119:103 KJV

He discovered that when he meditated on the words of the Lord, it made him feel good and satisfied. It was sweet like honey to him. In your spirit you can experience that "good taste" when the Lord is present.

To activate this aspect of taste, take a portion of Scripture that brings delight to you. Meditate on it and allow the "good taste" of the Lord's Word to fill you. Soak in this meditation until you feel satisfied, happy, and fulfilled.

When you are truly familiar with the good taste of the Lord, it is easy to discern a counterfeit.

I remember once a person was quoting a Scripture to me but was using it in an accusative and condemning way. It jarred my spirit. I felt myself rejecting the word immediately. It was like I was "spitting it out of my mouth" because it tasted terrible. Even though it was Scripture, it had the poison of accusation in it and I could not receive it. I love the Word and love the discipline the Word offers, but when the Lord is in it, it is good – it tastes "right" even if it brings discipline. This person delivered a word that did not have the Lord's signature "taste" in it, so I did not "eat it."

Not only does the Lord's Word carry a sweet taste, His presence does, also. You can discern the presence of the Lord by tasting its fruit. Does the presence you are sensing bring pleasure and delight to you? Does it create reverence within your heart? Does it draw you closer to His love?

As the apple tree among the trees of the wood, so is my beloved among the sons. I sat down under his

shadow with great delight, and his fruit was sweet
to my **taste**.

Song of Songs 2:3 KJV

The word taste also refers to partaking of an
experience. For example, Jesus said:

And thou sayest, If a man keep my saying, he shall
never taste of death.

John 8:52 KJV

Make a list of the things you have "tasted" or
experienced in the Lord. Perhaps your list might have
things like this:

I have tasted of

The Lord's goodness,

The Lord's kindness,

The Lord's life,

The Lord's strength,

The Lord's abundance, etc.

You can discern the presence of
the Lord by tasting its fruit. Does
the presence you are sensing bring
pleasure and delight to you? Does it
create reverence within your heart?
Does it draw you closer to His love?

TASTE TESTING

I was a judge at a cooking competition once. I had the privileged of taste-testing all the contestants' apple pies to determine the winner. I took a taste of each pie and then made an assessment.

We can do this with our spiritual sense of tasting, too. In things that you encounter day by day, intentionally taste and discern. Is it the Lord? Is it good? Does it bring peace to your spirit? Does it feel right? The more you taste, the more precise you will become in your discernment.

CHAPTER FIVE

THE SPIRITUAL SENSE OF SMELLING

In June 1994, our ministry hosted twenty-one days of powerful revival meetings named "Wind and Fire." For three months before the event commenced, we sought the Lord in prayer and intercession, inviting Him to move powerfully in our midst.

One day while praying with our intercession team in my living room, we began to perceive the distinct smell of fire. I was concerned that I had left a pot on the stove and it had caught fire, so I ran to the kitchen only to find that there was no smoke and no fire. The smell intensified, however, so I ran through each room of the house to attempt to find the source of the fire. After making the rounds a few times along with others who were with me, we could find no fire, and yet the smell was so real – so strong.

We gathered again in the living room and discussed amongst ourselves what it could be. We all smelled it. At that moment, through my living room window, we saw a fire truck driving slowly down the street. A thought immediately came to mind that a neighbor's home had possibly caught on fire and perhaps that was what we had smelled.

We quickly ran out the door and followed the fire truck down the street, noticing a couple of the fire protection crew knocking on doors making inquiries of the neighbors. I asked one of the firemen if there was an actual fire. He answered, "Well, we responded to a call on Badger Avenue but we cannot seem to find a fire; there does not appear to be any."

At that moment, I realized what had happened. The Lord was visiting our prayer meeting with a sign and wonder to confirm our "Wind and FIRE" event. The smell of fire was not from a natural fire, it was spiritual! He was having fun with us by sending the fire truck as confirmation.

A few days later when we were in the actual revival meetings, a smell of fire filled the church venue where we were hosting the meetings. Greatly alarmed, the janitor ran through the building, checking out each room to find which one had caught fire. He was perplexed that the smoke detector had not triggered, and for a safety precaution he actually wanted to vacate the premises in order to be on the safe side. I assured him that we did not need to vacate the building and that there was no physical fire. It was a sign from God.

The next three weeks of revival were glorious. We experienced many fragrances from the Lord in the meetings. We had the fragrance of roses, vanilla, frankincense, and orange blossoms. They would flow through the meetings as though Jesus was walking through and the folds of His garment were releasing fragrance. Many of the attendees could smell these. Some have asked in unbelief, doubt, and skepticism, "Why would God do something like that?"

I might not understand the full answer to that question, but one thing I have seen in response to the sign of His fragrance is that it causes those who experience it to be in awe of God. They grow more excited in His glory as they draw closer to Him.

THE AROMA OF YOUR LOVE FOR GOD

In the Old Testament, the priests would sacrifice gifts and offerings to the Lord on behalf of the people as an expression of worship and devotion to God. The

Scripture states that the aroma of the sacrifice was pleasing to God:

> And the priest shall burn all on the altar as a burnt sacrifice, an offering made by fire, a sweet aroma to the Lord.
>
> **Leviticus 1:9 NKJV**

Your love for Him today creates a sweet fragrance in the spirit. He loves your worship. He smells your love.

> Thy lips, O my spouse, drop as the honeycomb: honey and milk are under thy tongue; and the smell of thy garments is like the smell of Lebanon.
>
> **Song of Songs 4:11 KJV**

> While the king sitteth at his table, my spikenard sendeth forth the smell thereof.
>
> **Song of Songs 1:12 KJV**

The apostle Paul also acknowledged the sweet smell of the sacrifice of those in Philippi.

> But I have all, and abound: I am full, having received of Epaphroditus the things which were sent from you, an odour of a sweet smell, a sacrifice acceptable, wellpleasing to God.
>
> **Philippians 4:18 KJV**

I SMELL A RAT!

Your spiritual senses are your "discerners." Through the spiritual sense of smell, you can discern both good and evil. You have probably heard the saying, "I smell a rat." In other words, the "discerner" is discerning that there is something not good going on.

In the natural you can smell things that you cannot see. While on the mission field in Mexico, I walked into a room that smelled like something had died. I felt like vomiting. There was nothing visible so I began to look in the cupboards and under the furniture. In the cupboard under the sink, I soon discovered a large dead rat. It had been caught in a trap and I guess had been there for days. It was full of maggots and the smell was sickening. If you smell a rat, there probably is one around somewhere.

I have a particular discernment for cancer. I worked as a nurse for many years and in the course of my work I cared for patients dying of cancer. Cancer has a particular odor to it. I know that odor. Sometimes the Lord will release to me the spiritual odor of cancer to alert me to

Your spiritual senses are your "discerners." Through the spiritual sense of smell, you can discern both good and evil.

pray for someone and to help them battle that horrible enemy. When I smell that odor, it is very strong, but it is not in the physical realm. Others in the same room do not smell it. It is a spiritual sense.

I was ministering to someone a number of years ago and as I began to pray for them, I smelled marijuana. I looked at them and asked, "How long have you been smoking marijuana?" They were shocked and did not understand how I could know their "secret." I had been granted discernment from the Lord, using the spiritual sense of smell.

PRAYER FOR SPIRITUAL SENSE OF SMELLING

Lord, I pray that You will open up the spiritual sense of smelling for the reader of this book. May they smell Your presence. May their discernment grow in You through this wonderful spiritual sense.

CHAPTER SIX

THE SPIRITUAL
SENSE OF TOUCHING

In the physical realm, touch is very important and powerful. I remember being at a youth party as a teenager where they played a game in which they put all kinds of different things in a bowl and blindfolded you. You had to put your hands in the bowl and identify the items through the sense of touch alone. I won't share with you more details of that game, as some of it was beyond gross. Many of the participants were surprisingly accurate as they used this one sense to identify the objects.

In certain types of military training, officers blindfold the soldiers in the training exercise and have them attempt to find their way through a maze of obstacles by using their other senses. The sense of touch is very important in these exercises. They must feel their way through the maze, recognizing the presence of walls, textures, ground, people, and obstacles. In a real war, a developed sense of touch could possibly make the difference between life and death.

In a heavenly encounter, I experienced the Lord stretching out His scepter to me. The experience was very vivid, and to this day I remember what the scepter looked like. I saw it through my spiritual sense of seeing. I then heard Him (through my spiritual sense of hearing) say, "Touch My scepter." In the encounter, I reached out and touched it. As I did, I actually felt the tip of the scepter and I felt power flow into me through it. Even now, when I share the testimony of that encounter I again feel that power flow afresh into me.

The touch of the scepter and the feeling of the power that touched and filled my being was and is very real, but it is not physical – it is spiritual.

I have also experienced the touch of someone's hands (perhaps the Lord's) on my shoulders, and when I looked back there was no one there.

On another occasion I felt a spiritual wind touch my face and arm. I could literally feel the touch of the wind but there was no wind in the natural. My spiritual sense of touch was aware. In the Bible there is reference to winds (see Ezekiel 1), and Elijah was taken up to heaven in a whirlwind. (I wonder what that felt like?)

When you receive encounters like that, it is important to ask the Lord what the purpose is, because He is using it to draw you closer to Himself or to reveal something important. The hands on my shoulders took place when I was in a very vulnerable situation. That experience gave me confidence to know that the Lord was supporting me. The wind was to help me acknowledge the presence of angels that God had sent to minister to me.

> And of the angels He says,
> "Who makes His angels winds,
> and His ministers a flame of fire."
> **Hebrews 1:7**

Recently, I was on a prayer retreat. As I was soaking in worship, an angel came into my room. I "felt" its presence. I did not see it but felt it. The angel came closer and to my amazement it fed me food. That's right! I felt the food touch my lips and I felt the angel press the food into my mouth. It was spiritually tangible. I happened to be fasting while on that retreat, so I believe the Lord was feeding me food from heaven and that revelatory word entered me.

"He gave them bread out of heaven to eat."

John 6:31

Jesus said to them, "I am the bread of life; he who comes to Me will not hunger."

John 6:35

Then the Lord stretched out His hand and touched my mouth, and the Lord said to me, "Behold, I have put My words in your mouth."

Jeremiah 1:9

He touched my mouth with it and said, "Behold, this has touched your lips; and your iniquity is taken away and your sin is forgiven."

Isaiah 6:7

Then there came again and touched me one like the appearance of a man, and he strengthened me.

Daniel 10:18 KJV

CONVERGENCE

Sometimes natural physical touch and spiritual touch converge. For example, we are taught in Scripture to "lay hands on the sick and they will recover." This is referring to physically laying your hands on the sick, but within you is Christ's anointing. As a new creation in Christ, you have a "spirit man" body that has a "spirit man" hand.

Your spirit man is not just a blob in the midst of your belly. Your spirit man looks like you but it is spirit (I teach this principle in detail in the "New Creation Realities" lesson in *The Glory School*). In your physical hand is your spirit man's hand.

Therefore, when you lay hands on the sick (touch the sick), spiritual touch is also released if you have faith for this as you respond in obedience to the Word of God.

> And He touched her hand, and the fever left her: and she arose, and ministered unto them.
>
> **Matthew 8:15 KJV**

In the following Scripture you will see that when people touched the hem of the Lord's garment, they were able to receive spiritual blessing. The touch connected them to His healing power.

> And besought him that they might only touch the hem of his garment; and as many as touched were made perfectly whole.
>
> **Matthew 14:36 KJV**

Sometimes natural physical touch and spiritual touch converge. As a new creation in Christ, you have a "spirit man" body that has a "spirit man" hand.

FEELINGS AND IMPRESSIONS

The word *touch* can also mean an emotional feeling or impression. For example, your heart can be touched with compassion or empathy: "I was touched by your testimony."

> When Jesus therefore saw her weeping, and the Jews who came with her also weeping, He was deeply moved in spirit and was troubled.
>
> **John 11:33**

> Moved with compassion, Jesus touched their eyes; and immediately they regained their sight and followed Him.
>
> **Matthew 20:34**

Our ministry works with children who have been trafficked into the sex trade. The reason we are working in Thailand and Cambodia to this day is as a result of being deeply "touched" by the needs of the children there. We were touched by their needs and also touched by His love. One touch from the Lord on your heart can change your life. Many children are being rescued today because of the touch of the Lord that has motivated many to act.

INSIGHTS THROUGH TOUCH

I know individuals who are able to lay their hands on someone and through touching them they can discern health issues in their body.

I was at a meeting once where there was some spiritual activity going on in a corner of the room. It seemed that anyone who went into that space would get touched by the power of God. I went over to see what was happening and to partake of the action, and I noticed a tangible difference in the atmosphere as I drew closer to the area where the people were being touched. You could literally feel the presence of the Lord and it got stronger the closer I went into the area.

I found myself putting my hand up in the air to identify the boundary where I noticed the change. You could literally touch with your hand the boundary of the changed spiritual atmosphere. I had a sense that there was an angel standing in that corner and when people drew near to it, its ministry empowered them.

ACTIVATING

The best way to activate is to give yourself opportunities to explore the possibilities. Pray for the Lord to give you experience with your spiritual sense of touch. Perhaps you can begin by laying hands on people to see if you can feel or sense anything. Or when you are watching the power of God move, place your hand in its midst and see if you become aware of something from the Lord. The more you intentionally attempt to activate, the more sensitive you will become.

CHAPTER SEVEN

GROWING IN YOUR FIVE SPIRITUAL SENSES

ACTIVATION

Knowledge of a thing is not possession of it.

You have five spiritual senses that are for your use. But that doesn't mean you will automatically benefit from them. One of the ways you cultivate and develop natural senses is by reason of use. It is the same with your spiritual senses.

> But solid food is for the mature, who because of practice have their senses trained to discern good and evil.
>
> **Hebrews 5:14**

Take opportunity to use the senses God has given you. Every time you activate your senses, they will grow and develop.

PASSION

I have discovered that whatever I am passionate about, I will ultimately pursue. One of the ways to create and stir passion is to examine the benefits. What benefits would you enjoy if you developed your spiritual sense of: Hearing? Seeing? Tasting? Smelling? Touching?

Write down the benefits and review them. This will stir passion in you, and passion will usually empower action.

FOCUS

I have discovered that if I am working on too many things at once, I don't complete anything or do anything well. I would suggest intentionally taking one sense at a time and developing it. Sometimes when one sense opens up, others open up with it.

Focus is powerful. For example, if you were to focus on prayer, study, and activation of one of the senses for an hour or two a day over a course of a month or so, that focus would bring results. Try it!

PRAYER

The Scriptures teach us that when we pray and believe, we receive from God. Sometimes we have not because we ask not. Don't be casual about your prayers, rather be intentional and focused. Write out your requests and look up Scripture promises that support your desire. When you pray, believe that you will receive. Then thank the Lord daily for opening up the senses you are believing for. He truly is a God who answers prayer.

TEACHING

There are so many great teachers and teachings in the Body of Christ. Many who have had experiences in the Lord have prepared in-depth quality teachings on the subject they have matured in. You can receive from the best of the best. For example, when I was a young Christian learning about the prophetic, I took a

Passion and Focus are powerful. Stir passion by writing down the benefits of your spiritual senses. Consider focusing on one sense at a time and developing it through prayer, study, and activation for a month.
That focus will bring results. Try it!

five-month study on the gifts of the Spirit from a credible and experienced teacher and mentor, Mary Goddard, and activated the gifts regularly. (Please note: My mentor, Mary Goddard, has gone on to glory, but I have her original series on the gifts of the Spirit available in our bookstore at XPministries.com.)

Over the years, I met others who were proficient in the prophetic gifts, such as Graham Cooke, James Goll, Stacey Campbell, Cindy Jacobs, Bob Jones, Kim Clement, and Bobby Conner to name a few. I sat under their ministries also, reading their books and listening to their teachings. I attended their meetings and subscribed to the Elijah List so I could keep updated with fresh prophecies the Lord was releasing. As a result, I grew in the prophetic.

My teaching, *The Glory School*, is one course that will help you grow in your spiritual senses and spiritual encounter. I received the teaching through a 30-day visitation of the Holy Spirit. You can order this at XPministries.com.

There are many in the Body who have matured in the development of their spiritual senses and can help you. Go online and search them out. Get good, solid, biblical teaching from a variety of teachers. Study with an open mind and invite the Holy Spirit to help you sift through as you "extract the precious from the worthless," holding fast to that which is helpful to you. Today's Internet world has opened up so many opportunities. Our online Christian media network, XPmedia.com, hosts thousands of videos, messages and articles from various ministries that address subjects like this.

ASSOCIATIONS

If you desire to develop your five spiritual senses, hang out with others who do, also. If you belong to a church or have friends who are against the spiritual gifts or who are skeptics, this will thwart your growth in that area. Find others who are passionate to grow.

You can find those of like passion when you attend conferences or meetings that feature themes on the supernatural and the prophetic, or in churches who have developed a culture of embracing the supernatural.

Our Internet church, XPwebchurch.com, offers personal pastoral connection for each of our members. It has its own social media outlet for church members and many are growing in the supernatural as a result of the nurture they receive and the testimonies they share with one another.

RELATIONSHIP WITH HOLY SPIRIT

Jesus said that the Holy Spirit, when He came, would lead and guide us into all truth (see John 16:13). He is your Helper and Teacher, and He will never lead you astray. Develop a relationship with Him. Get to know Him. I teach a lesson on Holy Spirit in *The Glory School* that has blessed many. He is so wonderful and He is committed to your growth and development in the Lord. Do not lean on your own understanding – follow Him.

ACCOUNTABILITY

I personally believe in good accountability, especially for spiritual revelation. Have those in your life who will be honest with you and those whom you can submit fresh revelation to. This accountability partner or team (more than one) should be knowledgeable and credible in the things of the Spirit.

As a measuring tool, examine the fruit of your life and your experiences in the Lord. True encounters should produce humility, righteous and moral behavior, increased hunger, submission to others, and increased love for the Lord, in addition to other aspects of godly character. Jesus should be glorified in all.

As you move forward into new encounters in the Lord, remember that if you are in Christ, you already have these five spiritual senses. They are part of your new nature. You already have everything that pertains to life and godliness (2 Peter 1:3). You do not need to beg and plead for God to give you your senses. You already have them.

Believe that you have them and now – watch them unfold.

Dear Heavenly Father,

I pray for this precious one who has read this book. They are longing to have their five spiritual senses awakened and developed. I ask for You to empower them with Your Spirit, inspired revelation and insight, and authentic encounters as they begin a season of exploring the glorious blessings of their five spiritual senses. AMEN.

Let the journey begin!

Personal Notes

_____
_____
_____
_____
_____
_____
_____
_____
_____
_____
_____
_____
_____
_____
_____
_____
_____
_____
_____
_____
_____
_____

Personal Notes

About Patricia King

For over thirty years, Patricia has successfully coached, trained, and equipped believers to walk in their God-given callings. She has encouraged thousands through her prophetic ministry to see their potential in Christ and has walked through many challenging situations into glorious victory.

As a seasoned minister, businesswoman, and popular motivational speaker, Patricia King is the author of many books and resources, host of *Everlasting Love* TV program, founder and visionary of XP Ministries, and co-founder of the online Christian media network, XPmedia.com.

Her passion in life is to empower others to fulfill their dreams, visions, and desires, and to help those who are struggling to experience their breakthroughs. She is a skilled communicator and a gifted coach. Prophetic encouragement and ministry uniquely mark Patricia's coaching sessions.

For more information about XP Ministries and Patricia's itinerant schedule, go to XPministries.com.

Watch Patricia King's video teachings and television programs on XPmedia.com.

ARE YOU READY TO SOAR?

Do you long for deeper experiences with God? Would you like to press in for a more intimate relationship with Him? Well, He is longing for the same with you!

The Glory School builds Scripture upon Scripture to guide you deep into the reality of God and His divine Kingdom. You will receive insight and impartation that strengthens your faith and deepens your relationship with the Lord.

You will learn how you can experience the angelic realm, the third heaven, and closer encounters with the Holy Spirit. Get ready to experience the Lord in completely new levels of revelation and intimacy!

New! The Glory School manual and all 18 lessons in MP3 format are now available on a USB flash drive. The teaching is also available on CD and DVD (and can be ordered with the manual or without).

YOU'VE BEEN GIVEN *EYES THAT SEE!*

Do you desire to see into the unseen realm? Are you longing to gaze upon Jesus and His Kingdom? Then you need eyes that see!

Eyes that See will help you lay hold of the spiritual sight that you have been given in Christ. You will see in Scripture that the Lord has opened your eyes, and you will learn simple and practical ways to begin to practice seeing in the Spirit.

YOU'VE BEEN GIVEN *EARS THAT HEAR!*

Do you desire to hear what God is saying in this hour? Are you crying out for the Lord to speak to you about the deep mysteries of His Kingdom? Do you wonder what His plans are for your life? You need ears that hear!

In *Ears that Hear* you will come to know that you, too, can hear God's voice. There are simple practical ways to step into the prophetic and begin listening to what He is saying.

DECREE THE WORD!

Decree a thing and it shall be established. Job 22:28

The Word of God is powerful and it will profoundly influence your life. It accomplishes everything that it is sent to do. Patricia King wrote this book to help believers activate the power of the Word in key areas of their lives, including health, provision, love, victory, wisdom, family, business, grace, rejuvenation and many others.

UNLOCK YOUR LIFE'S FULL POTENTIAL!

Create Your World will empower you to frame your world and experience the kind of life Jesus died to give you. Extraordinary truths are presented with clear and simple guidelines to live a life of victory rather than a life of defeat.

As you read and apply the principles, your relationships, health, finances, and overall state of being will be supernaturally blessed by God!

UNLOCK THE POWER OF GOD IN YOU!

Tongues presents you with keys to accelerate your growth and maturity as a believer, help you enjoy deeper intimacy with the Lord and much more! Learn: why the empowering and gifts of the Spirit are so important in our daily walk and purpose as Christians; five amazing supernatural reasons you should pray in tongues; the role of praying in tongues in revival; how you can be baptized in the Holy Spirit and receive the gift of tongues, and much more!

SACRED TIME, SACRED PLACE – A JOURNAL

This beautiful imitation leather journal will help you develop a rich devotional life in your *Sacred Time, Sacred Place*. It includes practical guidelines for you to have a fruitful devotional time with Jesus, a plan to read the Bible in one year, and lined journal pages. Each page has a Bible Scripture at the bottom. The journal also has a ribbon so you can easily mark where you left off. Packaged in a gift box.

Additional copies of this book and other
book titles and resources by Patricia King
are available at:
XPmedia.com and XPministries.com

Wholesale prices for stores
and ministries

Please contact:
resourcemanager@xpministries.com

Most XP Publishing books are also available to
wholesale and retail stores through
AnchorDistributors.com

XPPublishing.com
XP Ministries